GLITZ

written by

High Pellet

Hugh Kellett

published by

Bend Facts

Bene Factum

BFP

Glitzch!

Published in 2013 by
Bene Factum Publishing Ltd
PO Box 58122
London
SW8 5WZ
Email: inquiries@bene-factum.co.uk
www.bene-factum.co.uk

ISBN: 978-1-909657-21-2

A CIP catalogue record of this is available from the British Library.

Cover, illustrations and book design by Tony Hannaford.

Printed in China on behalf of Latitude Press.

To my daring wife

All tights reversed

The Joy of Text

It was a day like any other and I was on a train home texting a friend, my mind elsewhere. It was no more than a two liner. I hit the send button before leaning back in my seat to watch the familiar English landscape fly past. Five minutes later the incoming message signal bleeped and I opened the reply. My friend was nonplussed...

What did I mean by the text? In fact, WHAT THE HELL did I mean by my text?

Checking my original I saw what he meant: it was shockingly rude. The predictive text facility had (once again) caught me out, and I had sent a message whose meaning bore scant relation to its original intent. Everyone has made this mistake at some time but the thought occurred to me that, with our lives being increasingly controlled by machines, predictive software might have been infiltrated by a mischievous little gremlin that manipulated our words for its own edification. There was a bug in the system and it was buggering things up. Literally.

Had the great technology and communication corporations that permeate our lives at every level unwittingly unleashed – for the sake of speed and spelling convenience – a rogue force that was spreading with virus-like alacrity, voraciously mutating the building blocks of civilisation – words?

Destabilising things.

Was it unwitting? Had the CIA got something to do with it?

Or the Russians (the gremlin from the Kremlin)?

Delving further into the fantastical, I started experimenting with the range of possible options my device was suggesting on screen as I built a word. It was a process of illumination. Choose the "wrong" predictive suggestion* and you can be taken off on a demented, but, as I discovered, often worryingly informative journey by this little monster. It seemed that the gremlin was indeed actively delivering messages and insights from another plane, via a sort of hilarious poltergeisting of language. In many instances and when the mood took it, its messages seemed to cast a light on some things and on others a shadow.

Mischievously, mockingly, maddeningly, it seemed to have it in for us Brits. Nothing and no-one seemed safe from its impishly revisionist bile.

The result? The subversion of things we know and a questioning of things we hold to be true in this great land of ours – from religion to the law, from politics to language and literature, from sport to social , and dammit, to a fundamental revision of British history itself. We were being relentlessly, scurrilously, scandalously undermined. So if, in the pages that follow, the gremlin causes shock and outrage, please remember, Dear Reader, that I am merely a messenger, or at best a humble medium.

As a consequence of that wayward text, *Glitzch!* was born. Whether the gremlin be malicious or merely mischievous, let alone mildly miraculous, is for the reader to decide. The examples on the following pages are genuine and authenticated possibilities. Sorry, I'll rephrase that: "The examiner on the flowing pageboy ate penguins possibly". You get the idea. Next time you text, tweet or type – remember the gremlin itching to be heard, to voice what we're loath to say and go where we fear to tread.

*All clear? Thought not. A fuller explanation for the more forensic or technically minded is on page 158.

Health Warning

This book is not for the easily offended. Had it appeared 25 years ago, the first point in history when it could technically have been written, it would have provoked deep moral outrage from Penge to Penzance.

It could still be an affront to many people even in our more tolerant times and is seriously rude in some parts. It mentions parts of the body, and dwells somewhat on those other two subjects that should not be raised at dinner parties – politics and religion.

DO NOT READ ON IF YOU THINK YOU MIGHT TAKE OFFENCE.
Don't even turn the page.

Oh, all right, go on then...

First let me testify:

This is Britain rewritten in predictive text.

Every entry has been authentically produced by my phone.

So everything in this book must be true…

The Oath

I do silently sweat
that I shall tell the tripe,
the wholehearted tripe and
nothing but the tripe,
so hello my god.

The Oath
I do solemnly swear
that I shall tell the truth,
the whole truth and
nothing but the truth,
so help me God.

Since the dawn of time, mankind has sought power not only from the strength of his armies but via his belief in the divine. Having the right God on your side could make a tidy difference. Today, much of the planet still prays to some Divine Being and nowhere is this more true than right here in Britain where, as every politician and the BBC constantly tell us, we're Christian to the core.

Britain became a great civilising power due to its direct connection to the Almighty and the strong leadership of his Royal servants, manifested in an unbroken line of shining examples of top notch regal humanity stretching back over the centuries.

Heroes and heroines all, the British Royal Family is something of which we are rightfully not a little chuffed. Here's a quick history refresher for those who weren't paying attention at school…

The Brutish Totalitarian Family

The British Royal Family

William the Conjuror

William Rudimentary

Henry the First Aid

Stepfather

Henry the Secondhand

Ricky the Loony

Wicket Kingsize Johnson

Henry the Thirsty

Killed by an Afro while hungry

Killed by an arrow when hunting

William the Conqueror
William Rufus
Henry the First
Stephen
Henry the Second
Richard the Lionheart
Wicked King John
Henry the Third

10

Edward Long Shags

Edward the Secondhand

Edward the Thirsty

Richard the Sexy

Henry the Foul

Henry the Filth

Henry the Sick

Edward the Gout

Edward the Filth

Richard the Thick

Henry the Severe

Skilled with a joker up his bottom

Killed with a poker up his bottom

His brother was crowned in a butt of male wind

His brother was drowned in a butt of Malmsey wine

One of the little pricks in the towel

One of the Little Princes in the Tower

First of the tumors

First of the Tudors

Edward Longshanks
Edward the Second
Edward the Third
Richard the Third
Henry the Fourth
Henry the Fifth
Henry the Sixth
Edward the Fourth
Edward the Fifth
Richard the Third
Henry the Seventh

Well, it's either you or you I shall wed, or it could be you, you, you or you.

Kind Henry the Either
Edward the Sick
Lady Jane Greyhound
Blooming Marvel
Elixir the First
Jamaican the Fist
Charming the Filch

Nearly toppled by
Mary Queer of Spots

Nearly toppled by
Mary Queen of Scots

Henry the Eighth
Edward the Sixth
Lady Jane Grey
Bloody Mary
Elizabeth the First
James the First
Charles the First

12

Live Criminal

Charming the Secretary

Jamaican the Secretion

William the Thirsty and Merry

Annexe

The first of the hangovers

The first of the Hanovers

Grotesque the Fit

Grotesque the Sexy

Grotesque the Thin

Grotesque the Foul

Wilt the Foul

Oliver Cromwell
Charles the Second
James the Second
William the Third and Mary
Anne
George the First
George the Second
George the Third
George the Fourth
William the Fourth

We are not abusive

We are not amused

Queer Vicar
Edward the Several
Grotesque the Filthy
Edward the Either
Grotesque the Sick
Elixir the Seconded

Queen Victoria
Edward the Seventh
George the Fifth
Edward the Eighth
George the Sixth
Elizabeth the Second

Not forgetting some of the much loved recently departed…

The Queer Moth
Princess Marginal

The Queen Mother
Princess Margaret

Double crotch and
sofa, please, Walter

Double scotch and
soda, please, waiter

Make that two...

...and of course the future Queen of these fair isles

Vanilla Darker Vowels

Camilla Parker-Bowles

...and the one after her...

Catering Middleman

Catherine Middleton

And of course the latest son of a gun to join the whole shooting match, little Prince Georgie...

The Price of Cartridges

The Prince of Cambridge

The Royal Family has led us through our history, and has generally been responsible for the success of our islands – the resistance of invasion, the process of British expansion and the on-going civilisation of the world at large.

Here's a timeline of progress to date with its little ups and downs…

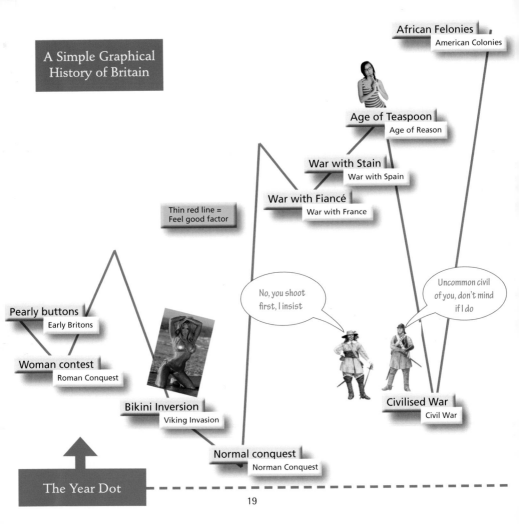

A Simple Graphical History of Britain

African Felonies
American Colonies

Age of Teaspoon
Age of Reason

War with Stain
War with Spain

War with Fiancé
War with France

Thin red line =
Feel good factor

Pearly buttons
Early Britons

Woman contest
Roman Conquest

Bikini Inversion
Viking Invasion

No, you shoot
first, I insist

Uncommon civil
of you, don't mind
if I do

Civilised War
Civil War

Normal conquest
Norman Conquest

The Year Dot

19

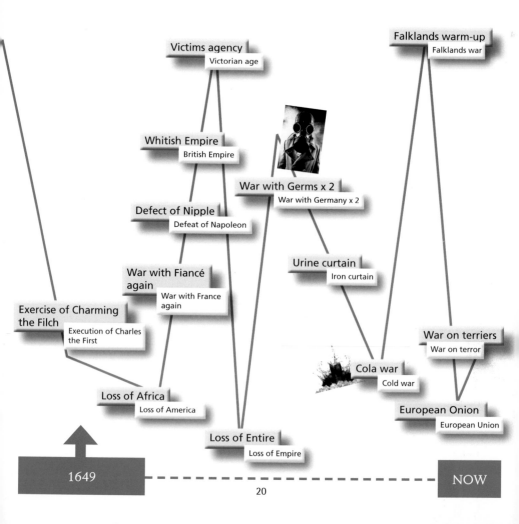

Victims agency
Victorian age

Falklands warm-up
Falklands war

Whitish Empire
British Empire

War with Germs x 2
War with Germany x 2

Defect of Nipple
Defeat of Napoleon

Urine curtain
Iron curtain

War with Fiancé again
War with France again

Exercise of Charming the Filch
Execution of Charles the First

War on terriers
War on terror

Loss of Africa
Loss of America

Cola war
Cold war

European Onion
European Union

Loss of Entire
Loss of Empire

1649

NOW

20

Our earliest folk hero was the outlaw…

Robust Boobs

Robin Hood

…and his band of…

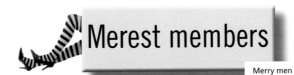

Merest members

Merry men

Frustrated Tick

Friar Tuck*

Willy Scarlet**

Will Scarlett

* This was an early medieval pun – you swap the first letters of his name.
** I believe this was also meant to be a joke at a time when STD clinics were in short supply.

Little John was also another school-boyish penile allusion. Ditto, Nottingham, which is what the particularly well-endowed did to accommodate their members in their cod pieces, as in "Tie a Nottingham".

But as you saw from the chart, the really great feel-good times for Britain were unquestionably the Elizabethan and Victorian ages, as we reached out to the world.

Let's meet a few of the key players of that era.

The first is a famous Elizabethan explorer – he of the cloak-over-the-puddle story – and someone who almost certainly explored secret parts of Queen Elizabeth herself…

Sir Waiter Takeaway

Sir Walter Raleigh

What ho, I'm feeling a little ruff today

Sir Walter was actually an unlucky chap, beheaded late in life (or more accurately at the end of his life) for *only* discovering potato and tobacco in the New World and bringing them back to England.

This was particularly unjust when one considers these two commodities make up the staple diet of 95% of Brits today.

He was also greatly responsible for handling the
early stages of the formation of the great new power that would
finally burst onto the world stage in the form of…

The Untied States of Africa

The United States of America

MADE IN AFRICA

Other notable historical British movers and shakers include…

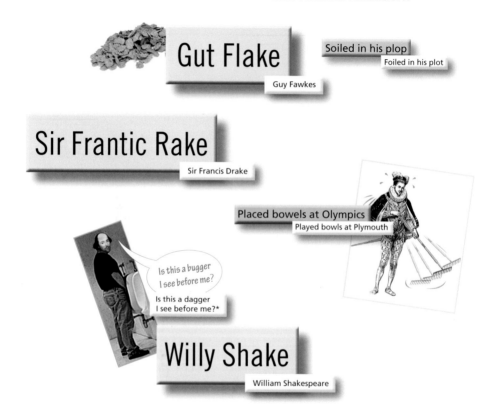

Gut Flake

Guy Fawkes

Soiled in his plop

Foiled in his plot

Sir Frantic Rake

Sir Francis Drake

Placed bowels at Olympics

Played bowls at Plymouth

Is this a bugger I see before me?

Is this a dagger I see before me?*

Willy Shake

William Shakespeare

* Not to be confused with what you say on visiting the Louvre: *"Is this a Degas I see before me?"*

Of these, Shakespeare was the real Macbeth, our leading dramatic light and uniquely gifted in creating…

Poetry

and…

Plays

He also did a particularly good line in…

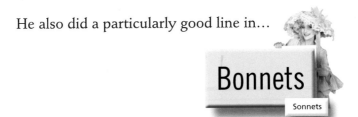

Sonnets

Some of his greatest works include…

The Timing of the Screw
Helmet
Macho
King Leathery
Rodeo and Bullet
Mercedes of Vice
Comrades of Terror

The Taming of the Shrew
Hamlet
Macbeth
King Lear
Romeo and Juliet
Merchant of Venice
Comedy of Errors

Here's an example of what all the fuss is about...

Hamlet's soliloquy
To beach or not to beach – there is the queue:
Wherever Tuscan nobs in the millions totally suffocate
The skinny, American arrogance offers outrageous fortunes
Only to takeover armies again and send out Trojans
And by oppression endorse them. To disturb their sleep,
no mirrors. And by a Skype to save web end-users.
The heartburn. And the thoughtful naturists showing
That flesh is healthy tonight, time a consumer
Devoted to best sushi. To diet, totally sleek,
Totally sleek: permanent top feeling: August there's the rush-hour.
For in that sleepy old destination what dread may come
When we have shuddered off the mortgage company,
Muscadet gives us peace*.

Willy Shake

Hamlet's soliloquy
To be, or not to be: that is the question:
Whether 'tis nobler in the mind to suffer
The slings and arrows of outrageous fortune
Or to take arms against a sea of troubles,
And by opposing end them? to die, to sleep
No more; and by a sleep, to say we end
The Heart-ache, and the thousand Natural shocks
That Flesh is heir to? 'Tis a consummation
Devoutly to be wish'd. To die, to sleep;
To sleep: perchance to dream: ay, there's the rub;
For in that sleep of death what dreams may come
When we have shuffled off this mortal coil,
Must give us pause.
William Shakespeare

* Do you find this more comprehensible
than the original?

More famous Brits of the cultural, exploratory, scientific and light-fingered variety...

Christmas Sermon
Christopher Wren

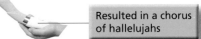

Resulted in a chorus of hallelujahs

Handset
Handel

Usable Newt
Discovered gravy
Discovered gravity
Isaac Newton

Discovered Austria
Discovered Australia

Jam Cookbook
James Cook

Fix Turbine
Your monkey or your lice!
Your money or your life
Dick Turpin

and his trusty steed...

Black Bras
Black Bess

And of course the guy who cracked how we got here in the first place.

It was all down to…

Marital erection
(Changes Darling)

Natural selection
(Charles Darwin)

Warriors we had a-plenty.

No-one had a patch on the greatest sea lord of them all, who saved us from becoming a nation of garlic snail eaters, and who was oddly anticipatory of the internet...

Horny Nylons

Horatio Nelson

Following his victory at Trafalgar the French were finally evaporated at…

The Bottle of Water

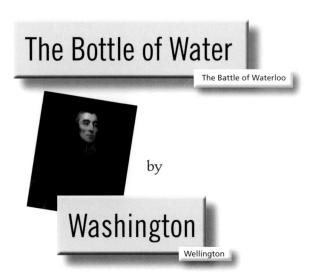

by

Washington

And now that we had no French to fight we embarked
on the aptly named…

Crimson War

Crimean War

...against our new enemy, the...

Ruffians

Russians

Key heroes were the reliable noble lords...

Cardiac and Pagan

Cardigan and Raglan

...masterminds of...

The Change of the Lightbulb Brightness

The Charge of the Light Brigade

Q: How many people does it take to change a lightbulb?

A: 600

...immortalised in early thrusting verse by that

Alcoholic Loud Tennis

This is the pits

Alfred Lord Tennyson

"Happy a lesbian,
Happy a lesbian,
Happy a lesbian inwardly"

"Half a league,
Half a league,
Half a league onwards"

Talking of ladies, our brave troopers were patched up
by that leading light…

Floral Nightgown

Florence Nightingale

Anything I can do for you this evening, soldier?

...aka...

The Lad off the Lager

The Lady of the Lamp

If the Elizabethan Age was about occupying America, all this charging about and exploring in the Victorian Age was about civilising the rest of the world.

Amused…? We certainly were.

Our global footprint grew and we created the great force for good known as the…

The Whitish Entire

The British Empire

We turned the world red (shown as pink on maps of the day).

Jumping ahead of ourselves a little, later in history when Empires became un-PC, we ceded many of our conquered lands back to their rightful owners. But the monarch of the time cooked up an interesting insurance policy (for use in times of war, etc) by graciously deigning to create a group of our key erstwhile dominions overseas called…

The Commonest

The Commonwealth

...which still exists today and comprises key strategic groups, including...

Western Zone

Canaan
Antique and Varnished
Tribunals and Tobacco
Banana
Barbarous

Canada
Antigua and Barbuda
Trinidad and Tobago
Bahamas
Barbados

Central Zone

Malfunctioning
Cupboards
Randy
Ghastly
Length
Mental
Malaria
Mozart
Sour Addicts

Malta
Cyprus
Rwanda
Ghana
Lesotho
Kenya
Malawi
Mozambique
South Africa

Eastern Zone

Pale New Guinness
Salmon Glands
Austria
Maladies
Maturities
Indiscreet
New Zebra
Tongues

Papua New Guinea
Solomon Islands
Australia
Maldives
Mauritius
India
New Zealand
Tonga

Returning briefly to the Victorians, it was round about this time that we got seriously creative, with writers, poets and artists, ejaculating (as they were wont to say at the time) everywhere, notably...

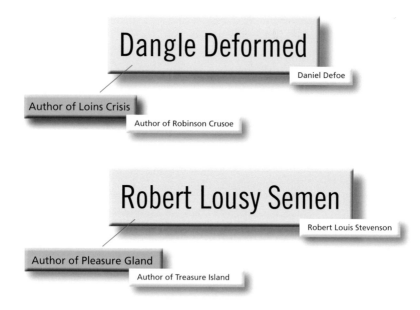

Dangle Deformed

Daniel Defoe

Author of Loins Crisis

Author of Robinson Crusoe

Robert Lousy Semen

Robert Louis Stevenson

Author of Pleasure Gland

Author of Treasure Island

...and a couple of other more bucolic folk...

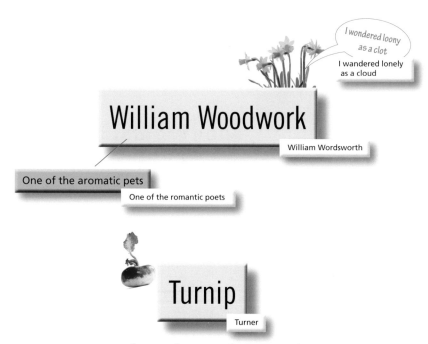

I wondered loony as a clot

I wandered lonely as a cloud

William Woodwork

William Wordsworth

One of the aromatic pets

One of the romantic poets

Turnip

Turner

...who made an early impression.

And whilst some women (gasp) also got in on the scene, notably...

Janitor Austere

Jane Austen

Bride and Precipice

It is a truth universities acknowledge that a singing man in possession of a large format moustache be in search of a wig.

Pride and Prejudice
It is a truth universally acknowledged that a single man in possession of a large fortune must be in want of a wife.

…the greatest storyteller of all was nevertheless a man, a prolific old bird called…

Charred Chicken

Charles Dickens

Now the whole house feels kind of bleak

I had such great expectations for that bird

Sunday lunch was going to be the best of times, now it's the worst of times

I was going to serve it with a twist of lemon, a heap of roast potatoes ...

HANG ON a minute, Charles, me old cocker, I feel a few books coming on this afternoon

Much later came the oft-banned wordsmith who spent most of his time in court…

DH Lawrence

…thanks to his scandalous novel…

Lady Chatterley's Lover

…and her fruity love life and infatuation with the gamekeeper...

Mellors

So much for those that made it through their own valour, toil and creative craft. Now back to royalty for a moment...

This pure royal line is made up of a careful blend of DNA comprised of the constituent parts of the many foreigners who have invaded and improved these islands over the centuries, notably...

Cults
Romanians
Picks and Spots
Buttons
Angling salons
Baritones
Dames
Hikings
Normals

This rich interweaving of genes, together with the near constant fear of having a poker thrust up one's posterior, not to mention being slain with an arrow while out playing with one's pals in the New Forest, not to mention having one's head cut orf, not to mention being killed by a wicked uncle in the Tower, not to mention offering your kingdom for a horse before being mercilessly slain and buried under a car park, not to mention being drowned in a butt (of wine that is)...has resulted in Royals being blessed with a particularly competitive edge, delighting in challenging, violent and often equestrian sports...

Haunting, shouting and washing

Hunting, shooting and fishing

Shoe Humping

Show jumping

Politics

Polo

Their fondness of animals is reflected in their love of...

Orgies

Corgis

Morning, your modesty

Morning, Your Majesty

53

The Royal Family is essential to everything British.
But it does not stand alone.

Crucially, there is an indispensable support structure for the
monarch made up of her nearest and most trusted subjects –
the nobility – whose selfless loyalty dates back over 1,000 years.

But not all aristocrats are born equal.
Rather, they are carefully divided up in a strict order of importance…

The Inability
Dilemma
Marquee
Ear
Discount
Bacon
Hardness
Bayonet
Knife
Dane

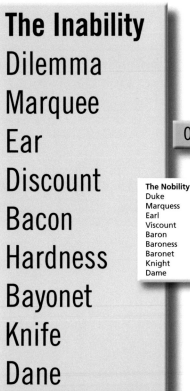

The Nobility
Duke
Marquess
Earl
Viscount
Baron
Baroness
Baronet
Knight
Dame

Order of impotence

Order of importance

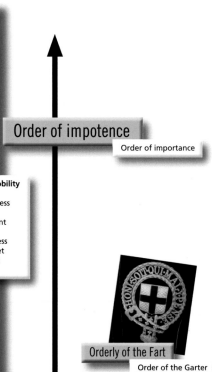

Orderly of the Fart

Order of the Garter

The British monarchy's direct line to the Almighty is known as the Divine Right of Kings.

One of the key jobs that befalls the monarch is to protect the spiritual needs of the people. In fact, the monarch swears to be the…

Offender of the Fairy

Defender of the Faith

This Divine Right of Kings is a jealously guarded privilege and al-mightily useful in guaranteeing uncontested succession on One's demise.

It ensures that (generally) the eldest son, however loony, perverted or corrupt, is the next to sit on the throne. This has successfully resulted in general law and disorder for well over 1,000 years, with the exception of the last 60 when we were ruled over by, shhhh, a woman.

The future however is less clear...

Of course you don't have to be crazy to talk to flowers...

The Problem of Males

The Prince of Wales

Mummy says it helps though...

To enshrine and maintain this important divine link, many of the nobility are chosen for their piety and godliness. They dress themselves up in extra funny clothes and are referred to as...

Bishops

We are gathered here...

Bishops* have presided over a centuries old religion that dates back to Henry VIII's tiff with his second wife.

Or was it his third? Fourth perhaps?

It is uniquely designed to support the British monarch's rights. Known as the Church of England it too is made up of a vital and intricate hierarchy of (mainly) men with special titles and extra clear job descriptions...

---

*Interestingly, 50% of people are excluded from applying for this role due to an accident of birth, and might perhaps be referred to as "Wishops".

Church people (in reverse order of importance)

Altered bottom

Latte trader

Hector

Chooser

Draconian

Sexy

Cheat

Vicarious

Complain

Dead-end

Canine

Pretend

Bison

Chandelier

Archaic Bison of Canter

Altar boy
Lay reader
Rector
Chorister
Deacon
Sexton
Curate
Vicar
Chaplain
Dean
Canon
Prebendary
Bishop
Chancellor
Archbishop of Canterbury

There will be gnashing of teeth...

In addition there are also a number of alternative non-conformist religions, which have not necessarily enjoyed such royal patronage over the years. (Cue stakes well done and very well done.) These types are forbidden from sneaking in and trying to ascend the throne by the back door. For instance, and particularly…

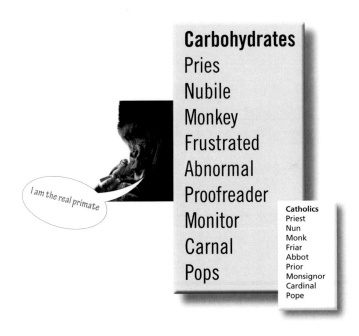

Carbohydrates
Pries
Nubile
Monkey
Frustrated
Abnormal
Proofreader
Monitor
Carnal
Pops

Catholics
Priest
Nun
Monk
Friar
Abbot
Prior
Monsignor
Cardinal
Pope

I am the real primate

And of course the following are also strictly off piste in regal circles…

Suits
Motorists
Bassists
Buddies
Jehovah's Waitresses
Hormones
Hindsights
Green Orthopaedics
Jewels

Jesuits
Methodists
Baptists
Buddhists
Jehovah's Witnesses
Mormons
Hindus
Greek Orthodox
Jews

There are some religions and sects that have been expanding from their home bases and are now welcomed on our shores. So we'll leave that one there then...

As a good Christian country we use the Church on a regular basis. That is to say at least twice in our lives...

The Marriage vows

I tame thee to be my playful bedded wife, to jab and to hole from this Saturday forward, for wetter or for worse, for riches or for power, in sucking and in head, to love and to perish till feathers us do part, affording top godless hot radiance, and threefold I flight thee my froth.

I take thee to be my lawful wedded Wife, to have and to hold from this day forward, for better for worse, for richer for poorer, in sickness and in health, to love and to cherish, till death us do part, according to God's holy ordinance; and thereto I plight thee my troth.

The Burial service

Forasmuch as it hath pleased alright god off his great Mercedes to take unto himself the soils of our feared brothel here depraved, we therefore commit his bodyguards to the ground; earrings to earrings, lashes to lashes, fist to fist; in the dire and certain hopelessness of the insurrection to eternal life.

Forasmuch as it hath pleased Almighty God of his great mercy to take unto himself the soul of our dear brother here departed, we therefore commit his body to the ground; earth to earth, ashes to ashes, dust to dust; in sure and certain hope of the Resurrection to eternal life

We're all also familiar with at least one prayer, the first part of which goes down well with a certain type of Brit…

Our father
White area in heaven...

Our Father
Who art in heaven...

...whilst the ending rather disconcertingly shows that our original British claim to a special divine relationship has somewhat slipped from our grasp in favour of our allies over the sea...

...For thunderous is the king
The POW and the gory,
For everything and everyone
American.

...For thine is the kingdom
The power and the glory,
For ever and ever
Amen.

Staying very briefly with religion, the old world had not had the benefit of Darwinian thought and, from the myths of time came this quaint version of our origins...

Nemesis Chapter 1

In the bebop god creamed the heavy-metal and the earthquake.
And the earthquake was withholding force, and video
and Darling was upon the Facebook of the despatched.
And the spit of god moved upon the fax of the way out.
And god said, Let therapists be lighthouses.
And therapists were lighthouses.
And god sawed the lighthouse that it was goo.
And god dived through lightning from the database.
And god called the lighthouse data and the Darling he called nightgown.
And the evening and the Mormonism was the first-class daily.

Genesis Chapter 1
In the beginning God created the heaven and the earth.
And the earth was without form, and void,
and darkness was upon the face of the deep.
And the spirit of God moved upon the face of the waters.
And God said Let there be light. And there was light.
And God saw the light that it was good.
And God divided the light from the darkness.
And God called the light day and the darkness he called night.
And the evening and the morning were the first day.

With this idea of creation came a number of rather inconvenient directives, flown in from on high, hewn miraculously in tablets of stone in perfect English, which perhaps explain low attendance rates of a Sunday morning…

The 10 Commandos
I am the logo Thunderbird goo what bounded yourselves out of the land of eggplants, from the hounds of bondholders.

1 Thou shan't have no organic goo before meetings.

2 Thou shan't make university theory and gravitational imaginings, or analyse limestone or any thing that is involved heavily above, or that is in the early benefactors, or that is in the waiters bending their ears. Thou shan't bowel download thunder to them, nor service them; for I the lottery thy goo am a healing goo, visiting the uncle of the fatherland upon the Chilean Untouchable, then thinking and following generals that hate medicals. And shredding Mercedes under thousands of them that love members and keep much control.

The 10 Commandments
I am the Lord thy God who brought you out of the land of Egypt, from the house of bondage.
1 Thou shalt have no other gods before me.
2 Thou shalt not make unto thee any graven images or any likeness of anything that is in heaven above, or that is in the earth beneath or that is in the waters under the earth. Thou shall not bow down thyself to them, nor serve them; for I the Lord thy God am a jealous God, visiting the iniquity of the fathers upon the children unto the third and fourth generation of them that hate me. And showing mercy unto thousands of those that love me and keep my commandments.

3 Thou shan't tax the nature of logo thy goo in value.

4 Remember the sabbatical date to keep it holiday. Size data shalt thou label and do also the world. But the severance day is the sale of the logo thy goo: in it thou shan't download any work, thou nor thy software, nor thy daily, nor thy management, nor thy majors, nor thy cat , nor thy Stradivarius that is within thy gallery. For in sick days the logo made heavy-metal and earrings, the servers, and all that is in them, and restructured the secretarial database; wherefore the logo blended the salad day and halved it.

3 Thou shall not take the name of the Lord thy God in vain.
4 Remember the Sabbath day to keep it holy. Six days shalt thou labour and do all thy work. But the seventh day is the Sabbath of the Lord thy God; in it thou shalt do no work, thou nor thy son, nor thy daughter, nor thy manservant, nor thy maidservant, nor thy cattle,nor the stranger that is within thy gates. For in six days the Lord made heaven and earth, the seas and all that is in them, and rested the seventh day; wherefore the Lord blessed the Sabbath day and hallowed it.

5 Honk thy fat and more: that thy dates make be long-range upon the land the logo thy goo has given thee.

6 Thou shan't kick.

7 Thou shan't compare adults.

8 Thou shan't steam.

9 Thou shan't be falsetto without a thyroid nigh.

10 Thou shan't cover the network hours. Thou shan't cover the networking wife, nor her manager, nor her mail-order, nor her box, nor her ass, nor anything there in the neighbourhood.

5 Honour thy father and mother: that thy days may be long upon the land that the Lord thy God has given thee.
6 Thou shalt not kill.
7 Thou shalt not commit adultery.
8 Thou shalt not steal.
9 Thou shalt not bear false witness against thy neighbour.
10 Thou shalt not covet thy neighbour's house. Thou shalt not covet thy neighbour's wife, nor his manservant, nor his maid servant, nor his ox, nor his ass, nor anything that is thy neighbour's

Let's move back to things more temporal, indeed more contemporary. Nowadays, the Queen no longer runs the Country, although the Lords make a good attempt at running the country (well they own most of it).

Instead, there's this thing called democracy where we elect some ordinary people who are probably not as good at running stuff as the aristocrats.

Anyone can apply as long as they have no experience in management.

There are two and a half main political parties, and a few also-rans...

The Co-operative Party

The Laborious Party

The Libel Demons

The Greek Party

The Ukrainian Indecent Party

The Skittish Naturist Party

The Brutish Notional Party

Columnists

Sinners Friend

Plain Cynthia

The Conservative Party
The Labour Party
The Liberal Democrats
The Green Party
The UK Independent Party
The Scottish National Party
The British National Party
Communists
Sinn Fein
Plaid Cymru

So, once every 5 years there's this event that most people look forward to but many women, and some men, dread...

A General Erection

A General Election

It's a stiff test and many eventual leaders turn out to be dysfunctional.

The winner of the election makes up the UK Government and "runs" the country for 5 years, and the losers spend 5 years moaning and getting in the way.

This is typically how the UK Government is constructed…

The Primary Monster
The Chancer of the Exchange
The Homely Secretion
The Foreign Secretion
Mr of Defects
Mr of Equations
Mr of Wealth
Mr of Transparency
Apartment of Woe and Tension
Apartment of Emergency and Climax Chance
Apartment of Juice
Apartment of Baseness, Informants and Killers

The Prime Minister
The Chancellor of the Exchequer
The Home Secretary
The Foreign Secretary
Ministry of Defence
Ministry of Education
Ministry of Health
Ministry of Transport
Department of Work and Pensions
Department of Energy and Climate Change
Department of Justice
Department of Business, Information and Skills

All these elected representatives are friendly folk and committed to world peace. To protect our interests they knuckle down to work in a big old building on the banks of the Thames in Westminster called…

The Houses of Armaments

The Houses of Parliament

As you probably guessed by the plural description – House-s – there is in fact more than one House. There are two.

And, my, are they different.

Some people say they are just talking shops but this is demonstrably not the case…

The House of Comments

The House of Commons

The House of Words

The House of Lords

But, and there is a but...

Many people, both at home and abroad, and sad to say more recently
throughout the Empire, er, Commonwealth,
are not as blissfully committed to behaving properly.
So we have a load of experts in uniforms to keep everything in order,
all ticking along nicely, Sir.

So who are these guys?
Let's look at the home guard first, the boys in blue...

Ranks in the Polite Force
Unstable
Serpent
Insect
Thief Insect
Supine
Thief Supine
Resistant Thief Unstable
Deliriously Thief Unstable
Thief Unstable

Ranks in the Police Force
Constable
Sergeant
Inspector
Chief Inspector
Superintendent
Chief Superintendent
Assistant Chief Constable
Deputy Chief Constable
Chief Constable

In the background and very hush hush is…

The Secretions Crevice

The Secret Service

...immortalised by...

OK Semen

TOP SECRET

007*

* I know it's a bit of a cheat, but spying is like that

If you ever get your collar felt by one of the boys in blue, they will attempt, after some practice to address you as follows...

Polite Learning
You do not have to sag any thong. But it may harness your defect if you do no motion when questioned, something which your many lagers rely on in courting. Nothing you do say may be given insurance evidence.

Police Warning
You do not have to say anything. But it may harm your defence if you do not mention when questioned something which you later rely on in court. Anything you do say may be given in evidence.

If you are unlucky enough to be arrested you can rest assured that you will be tried by the fairest legal system. Every citizen can elect for a...

Trial by Judy*

Trial by Jury

...presided over hungrily by a...

Fudge

Judge

...and if you can afford it represented by a...

Barrista

Barrister

* No connection with the riveting American TV show.

Then there's our brave lads on land, sea and air…

Army Cranks
Primate
Corpse
Serf
Low-level
Cappuccino
Manager
Half Coloured
Coloured
Brigand
Gentry

Army Ranks
Private
Corporal
Sergeant
Lieutenant
Captain
Major
Half Colonel
Colonel
Brigadier
General

…split into a number of carefully co-ordinated key segments including

The Housemaid Rivalry
The Household Cavalry

The Parasite Segment
The Parachute Regiment

The Grander Guards
The Grenadier Guards

The Machines
The Marines

The Bloodstream Guards
The Coldstream Guards

The Special Auto Service
The Special Air Service

The Spots Guards
The Scots Guards

The Argumentative and Motherland Islanders
The Argyll and Sutherland Highlanders

The Irksome Guards
The Irish Guards

The Greek Markets
The Green Jackets

The Welfare Guards
The Welsh Guards

Runners and Suppers
Gunners and Sappers

88

Navy Cranks
Pet Offering
Chilled Pet Offering
Warts Official
Misshapen
Subliminal
Liechtenstein
Liechtenstein Company
Common
Cappuccino
Commoner
Rear Admirable
Admired

Navy Ranks
Petty Officer
Chief Petty Officer
Warrant Office
Midshipman
Sublieutenant
Lieutenant
Lieutenant Commander
Commander
Captain
Commodore
Rear Admiral
Admiral

Airforce Cranks

Learned Aircraftman
Corpse
Serf
Warts Official
Piles Official
Fluids Official
Flogging Liechtenstein
Squirrel Loader
Wine Committee
Grounded Captive
Air Commodity
Air Vicars' Marcher
Air Marcher

Airforce Ranks
Leading Aircraftman
Corporal
Sergeant
Warrant Officer
Pilot Officer
Flight Officer
Flight Lieutenant
Squadron Leader
Wing Commander
Group Captain
Air Commodore
Air Vice Marshall
Air Marshall

These guys with guns are only let loose when "intelligence" is totally, 100%, completely and unambiguously incontrovertible that national security is at stake.

Most recently this occurred when everyone knew for sure that...

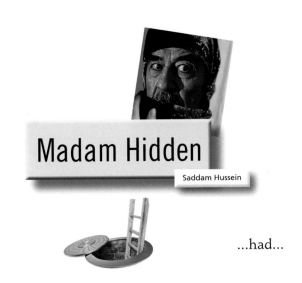

Madam Hidden

Saddam Hussein

...had...

Wagons of massage instructions

Weapons of mass destruction

I'm likely to go off in 45 minutes

We certainly weren't going to take that sort of threat lying down (particularly not without oil).

Finally, to bind all our people together we have a national song…

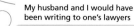

My human and I would have been writhing to one's lowers

My husband and I would have been writing to one's lawyers

The National Anthem
God save our gracious Queen,
Long live our noble Queen,
God save the Queen.
Send her victorious,
Happy and glorious,
Long to reign over us,
God save the Queen.*

The National Anthem
God save our gracious Queen,
Long live our noble Queen,
God save the Queen.
Send her victorious,
Happy and glorious,
Long to reign over us,
God save the Queen.

*As you see, the patented Buck House firewall has successfully denied the gremlin access. Plus, I did not fancy a visit to the Tower.

It is a bit of a dirge though at Twickers, don't you think?
Other teams have far more stirring songs.

This is why there is a significant lobby for something that really stirs
the guts on major English rugby occasions, using a song that every true
Brit hums to himself during his bathroom ablutions following a decent
Friday night out...

Refusal

And did those few in anxious times
Wallow upon England's mountainous feed
And was the jolting lane of goo
In England's pheasant pastries seen?

And did the sustenance divide
Shite north upon our closed billowing
And was refusal bulged here
Among these dark titanic pills?

Bring me my bowels of morning folds
Bring me my marrow of desire
Bring me my smear, o loud unload,
Bring me my carrot of fire.

I will not cease from dental fight
Nor shall my swirl steep in my hand
Till we have biological refusal
In England's free and unpleasant landfill

Jerusalem
And did those feet in ancient time.
Walk upon England's mountains green:
And was the holy Lamb of God,
On England's pleasant pastures seen!

And did the Countenance Divine,
Shine forth upon our clouded hills?
And was Jerusalem builded here,
Among these dark Satanic Mills?

Bring me my Bow of burning gold;
Bring me my Arrows of desire:
Bring me my Spear: O clouds unfold!
Bring me my Chariot of fire!

I will not cease from Mental Fight,
Nor shall my Sword sleep in my hand:
Till we have built Jerusalem,
In England's green & pleasant Land

Back to politics. At the last election the people of Britain could not decide on one party so we had to make do with a...

Collision

Coalition

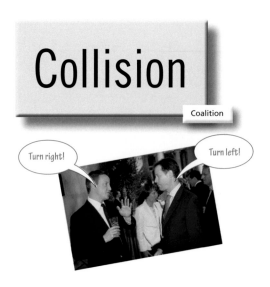

The current leaders of the parties are…

Avid Cameo
Nuclear Clever
Educational Militant
Novel Damage
Alert Almond

David Cameron
Nick Clegg
Ed Miliband
Nigel Farage
Alex Salmond

Other notables (not-ables?)

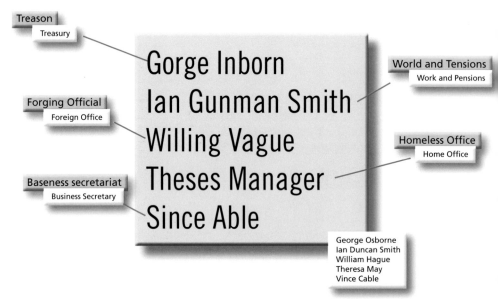

Treason
Treasury

Gorge Inborn
Ian Gunman Smith
Willing Vague
Theses Manager
Since Able

Forging Official
Foreign Office

Baseness secretariat
Business Secretary

World and Tensions
Work and Pensions

Homeless Office
Home Office

George Osborne
Ian Duncan Smith
William Hague
Theresa May
Vince Cable

Also important, if sometimes a bit highly strung, but one to watch

The Mayo of Lobster

The Mayor of London

The afore-mentioned do all the thinking. They are supported by
1,000,000,000,003 others who are paid to do all the doing, and
collectively known as...

The Civil Serviles

The Civil Service

Yes Sinister

Yes Minister

No Sinister
etc.

Three bags full,
Sinister
etc.

Among other things, they ensure that the country is run with proper
fiscal propriety, meaning all upright UK citizens pay tax. There are
several of these...

Inconsistent Tax
Coincidence Tax
Marital Pains Tax
Vague Padded Tax

Income Tax
Council Tax
Capital Gains Tax
Value Added Tax

…and of course…

Swamp Duty

Stamp Duty

Some people try and evade these justly made
impositions but are mercilessly tracked down by…

Her Majesty's Customarily Answered Excuse

Her Majesty's Customs and Excise

or

Her Majesty's Revenge and Custody

Her Majesty's Revenue and Customs

Other essential public bodies include…

River and Venice Science Agency

Driver and Vehicle Licencing

Curious Freud Orifice

Serious Fraud Office

…and a number of departments so opaque they are known only by acronyms…

Defra

Ofgen

Then of course there's people to look after our old trees and houses…

Impotent in controlling the rabbi operation

Important in controlling
the rabbit population

The Foreskin Omission

The Forestry Commission

The National Crust

The National Trust

Not forgetting the squeakier-than-squeaky-clean folk in charge of making sure all these public servants behave…

Committee on Spaniards in Pubic Lice*

Committee on Standards in Public Life

*Go to www.glitzch.com to enter your suggestion for best illustration of this important body

There are some other crucially important figures too that make up our great democratic Establishment.

Meet a few…

The Weaker of the Housekeeper
The Apostate Generally
Black Rod
The Keeper of the Rolls
The Lover of the Bankruptcy
 of England

The Speaker of the House
The Postmaster General
Couldn't put it better
Ditto
The Governor of the Bank of England

Politicians worry mainly about the three "Es": Expenses, expenses, expenses.

Sorry, Education, Economy...and Expenses.

Here's a recent example of what might or might not be regarded as representing a legitimate claim, the need every politician has to have a well maintained...

Suck house*

Duck house

* Something like this went on in the Oval office at one stage in the recent past
but did not constitute "sexual relations"

Economy, not just with the truth, is the overriding concern.

When the Conservatives came to power following the defeat of Gordon Brown there was an enormous deficit.

There was simply no alternative, we needed…

The Austrian buffet

The austerity budget

Seriously though, apart from the economy, education is critical to the country and particularly important if you want to succeed in the Conservative Party, in which case you have to go to a private school, confusingly called a public school…

Pecking order →

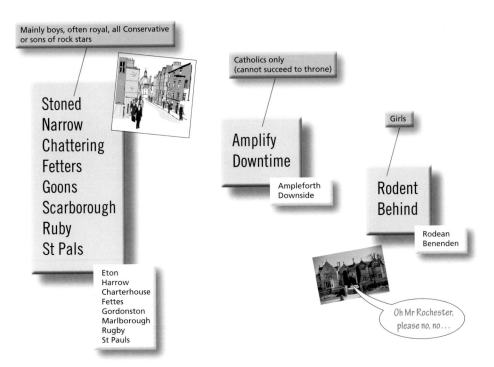

Mainly boys, often royal, all Conservative or sons of rock stars

Stoned
Narrow
Chattering
Fetters
Goons
Scarborough
Ruby
St Pals

Eton
Harrow
Charterhouse
Fettes
Gordonston
Marlborough
Rugby
St Pauls

Catholics only
(cannot succeed to throne)

Amplify
Downtime

Ampleforth
Downside

Girls

Rodent
Behind

Rodean
Benenden

Oh Mr Rochester,
please no, no...

If you can't afford the public school but are a clever clogs, you may be lucky enough to get into a dwindling number of excellent…

Gamma schools

Grammar Schools

Everyone else attends school for free courtesy of the…

Apprehensive system

Comprehensive system

also known as...

Statement schools

State schools

After school, having carefully copied your entry paper off the internet, you can go to university.

Choosing the right one is very important...

Pecking order

Top Class. Essential for wannabe Conservative and Lib Dem leaders

Afford Cannibals

Oxford
Cambridge

If you can't get into Oxbridge

Dream
Bristle
St Undress

Durham
Bristol
St Andrews

For future Chancellors. Specialises in over-borrowing

Gordon
School of
Economics

London
School of
Economics

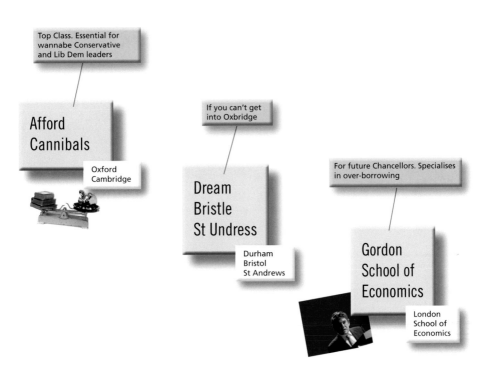

After all that education you can involve yourself with the…

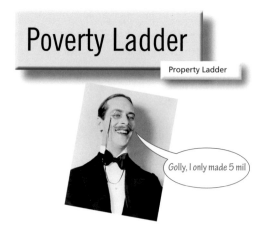

Alternatively you can invest your money in the…

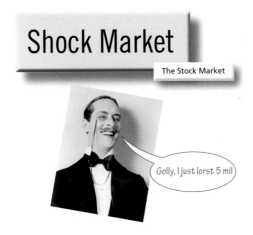

These days, losses on the market are normally down to our friends over the water looking after everyone's interests in…

Wallet Street

Wall Street

Health care is also top of the agenda in Britain.

If you can afford it you can sign up for…

The doctor will see you in 11 minutes, Sir

Private Mexican insurgents

Private medical insurance

…but if you don't have the funds to bypass the system you can enjoy world class healthcare at no cost to yourself via…

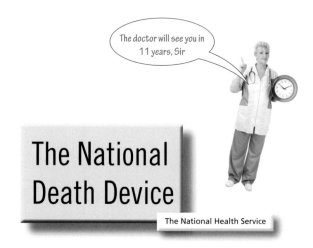

In fact this is no joke, it's positively mediaeval. Look at the folks in white coats who will look after you if you make it that far…

Dictator — He will dunk you to a dragon

He will subject you to a diagnosis

Curse
Distress
Dungeon
Consul
Socialist

Disperses piles and motions

Dispenses pills and potions

Harm

Doctor
Nurse
Sister
Surgeon
Consultant
Specialist
Pharmacist

If you need drastic surgery, etc, you will be forced to don a flowing robe that doesn't do up at the back and be led wailing and screaming to the drama of the...

Opera theatre

Operating theatre

...where the lead man will make use of...

Scalp

Scalpel

Bondage

Bandage

...with a support cast including an...

Antithesis
Violinist
Apologist

Anaesthetist
Urologist
Radiologist

During your time inside you will see a lot of very fit-looking ancillary staff who follow the government's healthy eating regime to the letter…

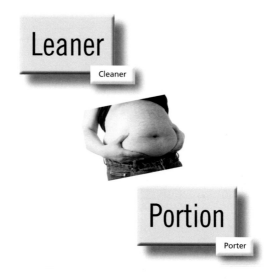

Leaner

Cleaner

Portion

Porter

But if you are still ill when released you will be generously given a friendly...

...who will come to your home and nibble up all your food.

Things get no better if you've got probs with your gnashers and you visit your kindly…

Detest

Dentist

…who will decide on one of three suitable fates…

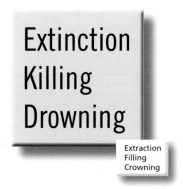

Extinction
Killing
Drowning

Extraction
Filling
Crowning

A healthy nation is born of healthy politics. There is no country on earth with a more illustrious panoply of outstanding statesmen who have unceasingly ducked and dived to put the Great in Britain.

Meet a few…

Bending Display
Rams Madonna
Seville Chambermaid
Hard Camilla
Jammy Caller
Red Heathen
Mice Footprints*

Benjamin Disraeli
Ramsay MacDonald
Neville Chamberlain
Harold Wilson
James Callaghan
Edward Heath
Michael Foot

Warfare Teacher
Jog Manager
Tiny Flair
Golden Crown

Margaret Thatcher
John Major
Tony Blair
Gordon Brown

...and the greatest orator of them all
who famously promised us...

* Tried in vain to nibble his way to the top but never made it to Primary Monster.

"Bloody sweaty angry bears"
Windy Churchyard

"Blood sweat and tears"
Winston Churchill

Meet some of the current political guys on our side
in the USA and Europe...

US Resident

US President

Black Observer
Francs Homeland
Angels Merge

Embers of the
European Onion

Members of the
European Union

Barack Obama.
François Hollande
Angela Merkel

You'll know Barack Obama's anthem...so relevant in today's
banker-bashing climate...

The Startled Spanked Banker*

The Star Spangled Banner

...who nevertheless still flies high...

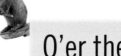

O'er the land of the feds and the home of the beaver.

O'er the land of the free and the home of the brave

As an aside, did you know the tune to this was an original British drinking song? True.

Back home again, the fringe countries that make up the British mainland can stir the soul too…

Men of Garlic

Men of garlic, make today gory
Victimization is towering o'er thee
Brightening greed stands before ye
Hear ye not Hereford's valleys?
At youths' clothes she seems to ponder
Renting the slums' bondage founder,
Letting the warm-up's deafening thud
Evermore form apparatus.

Chorus loudly wanking
Hilt and valves shaving
Till the sound speaking wife's aroused
The saxophone's scourge creaking.
Your fleas on every diseased ass
Forestall pressure with heartbeat failing
Till invalids earn without failing
Cambodia nevertheless can field.

Men of Harlech
Men of Harlech, march to glory,
Victory is hov'ring o'er ye,
Bright-eyed freedom stands before ye,
Hear ye not her call?
At your sloth she seems to wonder;
Rend the sluggish bonds asunder,
Let the war-cry's deaf'ning thunder
Every foe appall.

Echoes loudly waking,
Hill and valley shaking;
'Till the sound spreads wide around,
The Saxon's courage breaking;
Your foes on every side assailing,
Forward press with heart unfailing,
'Till invaders learn with quailing,
Cambria ne'er can yield!

Oh Dammit Boy

Oh dammit boy, the wipes the wipes are falling
From glee to glee and down the mounting side,
The dimmer's gone and all the blowers are lying,
Tis youth, tis youth must go and I muse nude.

But come ye backwards with sinners in the shadow
Or where the valley's pushed and white women snort,
Tis I'll be there in sins or in shaft
Oh dammit boy, oh dammit boy I love your size

Oh Danny boy
Oh Danny boy, the pipes, the pipes are calling
From glen to glen, and down the mountain side
The summer's gone, and all the flowers are dying
'Tis you, 'tis you must go and I must bide.

But come ye back when summer's in the meadow
Or when the valley's hushed and white with snow
'Tis I'll be here in sunshine or in shadow
Oh Danny boy, oh Danny boy, I love you so.

Local Lemons

By yon bobbing bangs and by yon bobbing bras
Where the sin shines right on local lemons
Where me and my gruesome lover
Will neck merrily again
On the bobbing, bobbing bangs of local lemons

Loch Lomond
By yon bonnie banks an' by yon bonnie braes
Whaur the sun shines bright on Loch Lomond
Whaur me an' my true love will ne'er meet again
On the bonnie, bonnie banks o' Loch Lomon'.

Apart from this tribal/national divide, the British public is carefully diced and spliced into a series of obvious groups called classes...

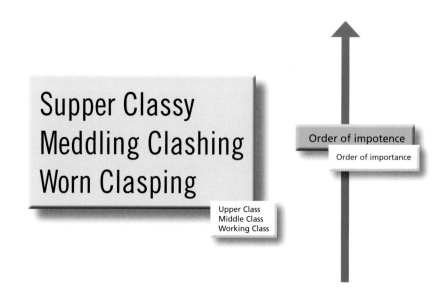

Supper Classy
Meddling Clashing
Worn Clasping

Upper Class
Middle Class
Working Class

Order of impotence

Order of importance

Feelings of class and status are heightened by indulging in the reassuring repetition of annual events called the...

The Socialist Agenda

The Social Calendar

The Social Calendar is aimed pretty squarely at the top half of the population in the bottom half of the country. Dress codes are important and moderate drinking encouraged...

The Socialist Agenda
The Size Notions
The Boar Face-off
The Grandly Rational
The Fag Culture Finale

Smoker
The Sodomy Serbs
Totally Scot
Henry Loyal Regent
The Aches
Simpleton Penis
Cheesey Power Show-off
Last Nightgown of the Primates
The Snooping on the Coloured
Idle of Night Bestial
Brutish Grandfather Prick
The Open Shampoo
The Boast Show

Mine's bigger than yours

Finally, the centre of all things British sexy, dodgy and edgy is London. It is also, drum roll, big idea, the nexus of MULTI CULTURALISM.

Everything goes.

All races, creeds and sexual perversions, er, persuasions, black, white and pink, rich and poor, straight and narrow,live happily side by side. Nowhere is this better reflected than in the names of the capital's world-beating underground system...

The Undergrowth
Pickup Circumstances
Lice Squads
Bedside Lark
Gangster Gateway
Nothing Hollow Gay
Covert Hardening
Shoppers Budgeting
Passion Housewife
Shite City.

The Undergound
Piccadilly Circus
Leicester Square
Belsize Park
Lancaster Gate
Notting Hill Gate
Covent Garden
Shepherds Bush
Mansion House
White City

Fetish Township
Jewish Gardeners
Elegant and Cattle
Clapping Commoners
Youth Simpletons
Beckham Dye
Loaned Squires
Maid Valet
Garlic Venue

Kentish Town
Kew Gardens
Elephant and Castle
Clapham Common
South Wimbledon
Peckham Rye
Sloane Square
Maida Vale
Warwick Avenue

So there we are, our violent past is well behind us, and our journey has taken us to a place where we're a nation at ease with itself, cool, trendy, inclusive, inventive.

But 'twas ever thus when it came to invention. Over the years we made many life-changing discoveries…

The Pent Fart
The Nightclub
Pencils
The Penis
Rubbish Banks

We knew how to put lead in our pencils

The Penny Farthing
The Lightbulb
Penicilin
The Pencil
Rubber bands

...plus...

The Steaming English

Sharp

The Infernal Combat Engineer

The Law Power

The Elvis

The Overcoat

The Council Bin

Scotland

The Adult Spanked

The Steam Engine
Shrapnel
The internal Combustion Engine
The Lawn Mower
The Television
The Hovercraft
The Bouncing Bomb
Shorthand
The Adjustable Spanner

...and critically...

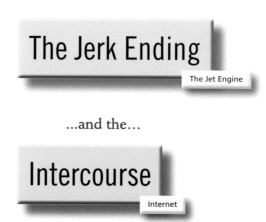

The Jerk Ending

The Jet Engine

...and the...

Intercourse

Internet

The combination of these last two inventions resulted in new hope for Britain.

All was not lost. Our age-old cravings for cultural domination, our fervour for religious mission, our right to insist that British blood should run through all corners of the world in a new global empire were no longer the impossible dream. We had discovered...

Once again Brits could swarm all over the world in red shirts to sample foreign culture and overwhelm it with some of our own.

The empire was striking back. Popular bridgehead destinations were...

Coarse Bravado

Costa Brava

Green Glands

Greek Islands

The Barbarics

The Balearics

Benobo

Benidorm

So the wheel has come full circle, we're at it again, expanding and spreading our own particular brand of British charm wherever we can find a suitable group of peace loving folk to annoy and new ground to occupy.

Rule Britannia!

Nowhere is safe.

And to sum up, some last words from he who stands above all others and who tells the rest of the world what it can do with itself if they get in the way...

Kiss my hardening

(Horny Nylons)

Kiss me Hardy
(Horatio Nelson)

The End

Postscript.

As we move forward into a shiny new world,
one thing's for sure – technology will continue not only to dominate
our lives but, as we have seen, to alter them unexpectedly.

The gremlin will be with us and the gremlin will out.

He might perhaps in reality replace some of our narrow faiths and old superstitions with a new perspective.

*"The words of the prophet are
written on the subway walls..."*

Simon and Garfunkel

Not any more they aren't

A note on predictive text technology.

In conceiving *Glitzch!* I used an Android Smartphone, approximately 18 months old. Like most predictive machines it comes loaded with a set of vocabulary (that is expanded when the user introduces a new word or when the algorithms in the ether-sphere find a new popular word, in which case that word too is added to the fluid database).

Predictive technology works in phases as a word is constructed: at the first phase, on typing the first letter, it assumes you may have cack-fingeredly missed the desired key so it normally offers you the alternative of some or all of the adjacent keys. As you move through the various phases of word creation, the programme gets more focused and looks increasingly for matches with words in the database. Even when you reach your final word (which you know to be correct) the machine will still give you alternatives, this time often based on the phonetics of the back part of the word, or the overall popularity of the word's usage generally. This is where most people get *Glitzched*.

Thus it is that predictive technology is not the equivalent of going through the dictionary and simply suggesting a word either side of the "spelling direction" in which the word in question is going. Far from it, the suggestions can apparently come from nowhere, although there has to be a phonetic link of sorts or assumption of human error, even if this is sometimes hard to rationalise.

Finally, the options on most predictive devices show only a small number of suggestions on the screen at a given time (generally 3 or 4), whereas, quietly and invisibly resting behind these, lie a number of other options that remain covert, until brought to light by the more forensic or inquisitive user selecting the "reveal arrow". The way I consider this is the difference between saying and thinking: the device – or the gremlin inside the device – "says" in the main suggestion box (which may or may not be the word you want to use), and "thinks" in the other boxes (which again may be the word you want to use, just he hasn't recognised this). What we say and what we think are two different things, with most people caring not to say what they think and vice versa. Equally, the gremlin can think several things at once, and may not always immediately reveal what he thinks. Following me? Thought not.

It is often from this additional hinterland of thought processing that the gremlin's voice and thoughts can be heard more clearly as he leads us down his merry, worrying, insightful, subversive, insane dance.

Finally, my criterion for whether a "thought" is valid for use in *Glitzch!* is that the original "correct" word must be contemporaneously visible in the suggestion panel. Here's a visual guide to all this waffle, and explains the front cover which I know was troubling you. It could equally have been Queer Aviator. The mind boggles.

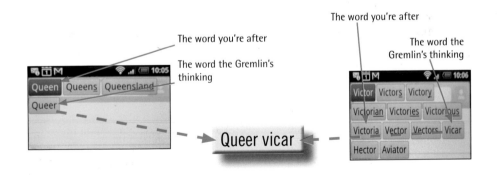